FOCUS ON

JAPAN

Mavis Pilbeam

Evans Brothers Limited

In memory of my parents

Published by Evans Brothers Limited
2A Portman Mansions
Chiltern Street
London W1M 1LE

First published in Great Britain in 1987 by
Hamish Hamilton Children's Books

© Mavis Pilbeam 1987

Design by Andrew Shoolbred
Map by Tony Garrett
Illustrations by Gillian Hurry, Linda Rogers Associates
Calligraphy artwork by Kyoko Read

New edition published 1991
Reprinted 1996 (twice)

Printed in Spain by GRAFO, S.A. – Bilbao
ISBN 0 237 51661 6

Acknowledgements

The author and publishers would like to thank the following for permission to
reproduce the photographs: Inez Cropley 12 (right), 17 (left); John Greenlees
cover; Susan Griggs Agency 11; Robert Harding Picture Library title page,
9 (left), 10 (bottom), 18, 22 (right), 26; John Hillelson contents page, 24, 30;
photograph through courtesy of the International Society for Educational
Information, Inc. 23 (right); Japan Foundation 10 (top), 19, (left), 20, 21, 31;
Japan Information and Cultural Centre, Embassy of Japan, London 6, 14, 15,
16, 17 (right), 22 (left), 25 (left); Port of Kobe Authority, London 7; John Read
19 (right), 28; Tony Stone Worldwide 13, 23 (left), 27; The Telegraph Colour
Library 12 (left); Janet Tregidgo 9 (right); Fraser Tweedie 8; by courtesy of the
Board of Trustees of the Victoria and Albert Museum 25 (right).

Cover The Gion Festival is one the most popular and
spectacular festivals in Japan. It is held in Kyoto on
17th July to commemorate a plague in AD 869. Crowds of
people line the streets to watch a procession of enormous
floats decorated with rich tapestries and life-size figures of
famous people from Japanese history. Teams of chanting
men pull the floats along on rollers. The noise is
unbelievable!

Title page A farmer and his wife in Hokkaido harvesting
rice using a small combine-harvester. Rice is planted and
grown in specially flooded fields called paddy-fields,
which dry out by harvest time.

Opposite Most Japanese people live in large cities where
space for houses is scarce, so more and more blocks of flats
called *danchi* are being built. This is a view of *danchi* in a
new town near Tokyo. Notice how people like to hang
their bedding out to air on their balconies in the morning.

Contents

Introducing Japan

Japan is a country of islands with many high mountains and huge, modern cities. It is in the eastern part of Asia. To the west of Japan lies a narrow sea called the Sea of Japan, across which lie Japan's closest neighbour countries, Korea, China and Russia. To the east lies the Pacific Ocean.

Islands and cities

Japan has four main islands, Honshu, Hokkaido, Kyushu and Shikoku. Nearly 125 million people live in Japan, and the country covers almost 400,000 square kilometres. However, four-fifths of the land is very mountainous so most people live and work on the flat land along the coast. Tokyo, the capital, lies in the biggest plain, the Kanto Plain. Other important cities are Osaka, a business centre, Nagoya, an industrial centre and port, and Yokohama, another famous port. The cities of Japan are crowded with houses and shops, offices and factories, but the mountains are very peaceful and beautiful, with many lakes and swift rivers.

The past

In the past, most Japanese people were farmers. Japan did not know much about other countries, except Korea and China. Over the centuries the Japanese developed a special way of life with their own customs and arts. Japan has always had an Emperor. However, from 1192–1868, there was also a powerful military leader, the Shogun. The most famous Shogun, Tokugawa Ieyasu, took control of the whole country in 1603. Then, in 1639, he closed Japan almost completely to the outside world; he feared the power of some European countries.

The present

However, in 1853, some Americans arrived and forced Japan to start trading with them. Several European countries joined in. Japan decided to learn more about these western countries and introduced new ideas from them. Gradually Japan changed. Today it is one of the world's leading industrialised nations. The Emperor is the head of the country and there is also a modern government system with a Prime Minister and Cabinet, and a Parliament, called the Diet, elected by the people.

The Japanese are still proud of their old Japanese customs, arts and way of life, but now they mix them with things from abroad like skyscrapers and hamburgers!

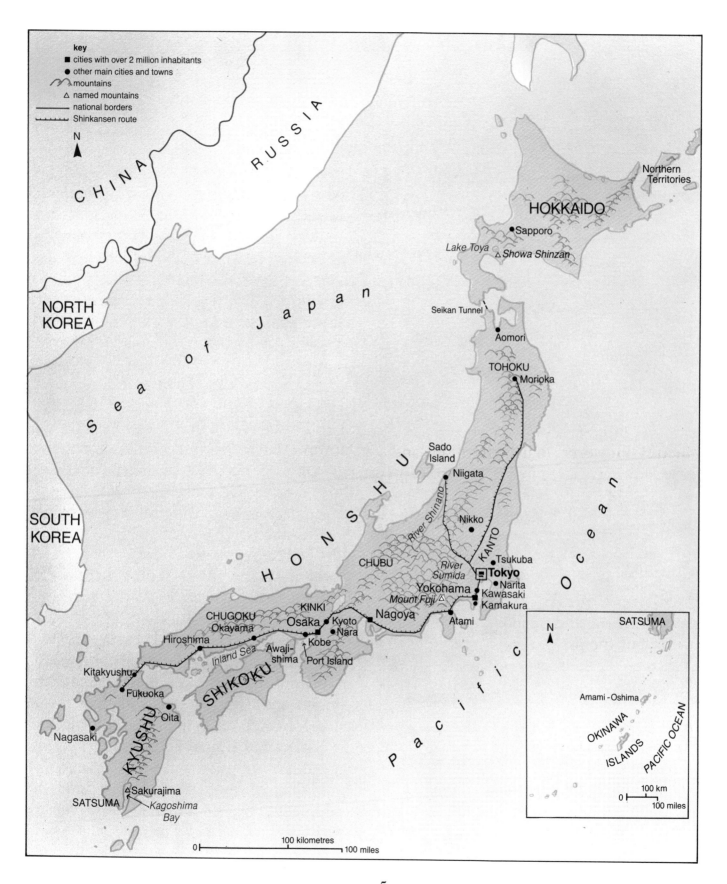

key
■ cities with over 2 million inhabitants
● other main cities and towns
⌃ mountains
△ named mountains
— national borders
⊤⊤⊤ Shinkansen route

N

CHINA

RUSSIA

Northern
Territories

HOKKAIDO

● Sapporo

Lake Toya ○

△ *Showa Shinzan*

NORTH
KOREA

Seikan Tunnel

● Aomori

Sea of Japan

TOHOKU
● Morioka

Sado
Island

● Niigata

SOUTH
KOREA

River Shinano

● Nikko

KANTO

CHUBU

*River
Sumida*

● Tsukuba

■ Tokyo
● Narita

Yokohama ●
Mount Fuji △
● Kawasaki
● Kamakura

KINKI

● Nagoya

● Atami

CHUGOKU
Okayama ●

Osaka ■
Kyoto ●
Nara ●

Hiroshima ●

Inland Sea

Kobe ■

Awaji-
shima

Port Island

SHIKOKU

Kitakyushu ●

● Fukuoka

● Oita

KYUSHU

Nagasaki ●

SATSUMA

△ Sakurajima

*Kagoshima
Bay*

P a c i f i c   O c e a n

N

SATSUMA

Amami - Oshima

OKINAWA

ISLANDS

PACIFIC OCEAN

100 km

0

100 miles

100 kilometres

0

100 miles

An island country

The Seto Ohashi Bridge 'hopping' across the Inland Sea linking the main islands of Honshu and Shikoku. This is the first to be completed of three sets of bridges.

Honshu, Hokkaido, Kyushu and Shikoku form a long narrow arc-shape, stretching 3,800 kilometres from north to south. Because the islands are narrow, most people live near the sea, so fresh fish has always been easy to get. The seas are very dangerous. More people are drowned through shipwrecks than in other country in the world. Until this century, however, the dangerous seas have also had their use, protecting Japan from attacks by other countries.

Besides the four main islands, there are nearly 4,000 small ones. Some of these, like Sado Island off the north-east coast of Honshu, and Okinawa, 500 kilometres off the southern tip of Kyushu, are big enough for people to live on. Others are just enormous masses of rock sticking out of the sea.

Tunnels and bridges

In the past, the only way to get from island to island was by boat. In recent years, the Japanese have been building bridges and tunnels to make travelling quicker and easier. The first islands to be linked were Honshu and Kyushu, with road and rail tunnels and a suspension bridge. Honshu and Hokkaido are linked by the Seikan Tunnel, a rail tunnel 54 kilometres long. It was opened in 1988 and took 24 years to build. The technology which was developed to build the Seikan Tunnel is now being used for the Channel Tunnel.

Port Island was opened in 1981 with a big exhibition. There were some unusual stands including a giant coffee cup and saucer! In the background are some ships alongside the quays with their enormous cranes. Port Island has the largest container port in Japan. The goods are packed in very big metal boxes called containers which can be moved easily on and off ships or lorries. A second even bigger island called Rokko Island is now being built next to Port Island. It was constructed in a different way so it was not damaged in the earthquake (see below).

Three sets of bridges are being built to link Honshu and Shikoku. The middle set of six bridges 'hopping' from island to island across the Inland Sea was opened to traffic in 1988. The Akashi-Kaikyo Suspension Bridge from Awajishima to Kobe has a central span of 1,780 metres, the longest in the world.

Another giant new project is the building of a route across the mouth of Tokyo Bay with a central bridge and two tunnels. It will probably open before April 1997.

Man-made islands

Because Japan is such a mountainous country surrounded by the sea, the Japanese have to think of new ways of making space. In some places they are actually building new islands in the sea. An example is Port Island in the Inland Sea, near Kobe. Kobe is a long, narrow city running along the coast with high mountains behind it. To make the island, the workers cut off the tops of several of the mountains. The rocks and stones were run by conveyor-belt to the coast, then taken out in boats and dumped on the seabed. Gradually the pile grew and grew until it formed a new island rising out of the sea. They built new factories and docks, houses, schools and shops on the new land. Unfortunately, Kobe City and Port Island were badly damaged in the Great Hanshin Earthquake (see page 8). Now the Japanese must rebuild them. Port Island is important for trade and industry, and they plan to use the docks and factories again by 1998.

In some places, such as Oita in Kyushu, instead of making islands, they just build out from the coast. Here, huge steelworks stand on the new land. So every year the coastline of Japan is changing its shape.

Volcanoes and earthquakes

Japan is in a part of the world which has many earthquakes and volcanoes. These can occasionally be dangerous, causing serious damage to town and countryside, so the Japanese have to study ways of predicting big earthquakes and volcanic eruptions. They even have earthquake drills (like school fire drills) to train people to act as calmly as possible if there is a big earthquake.

'Disaster drill' at a big store in Tokyo.

Certain areas of cities are left empty so the people can gather there safely in an emergency. Engineers have found out that skyscrapers with very deep foundations will not fall down during an earthquake.

Earthquakes

Most earth tremors are very small and nobody notices them. If there is a slightly stronger one, the garden wall may sway a bit and, in rooms at the tops of blocks of flats, pictures swing to and fro. On 17 January, 1995, a very severe earthquake struck the city of Kobe and Awaji Island. It is known as the Great Hanshin Earthquake. More than 5,400 people were killed. Many houses and office buildings were burnt or fell down. Roads and railways were destroyed, including the Shinkansen tracks (see page 16). This disaster shocked the whole country, and the outside world. But the Japanese are trying to learn from the experience. They hope to rebuild Kobe as a much better, safer city.

Japan has a special scale for measuring the strength of earthquakes. The strongest is number 7 on the scale. After an earthquake, people switch on the TV set to see what number the quake was.

Volcanoes

In Japan there are over sixty active volcanoes. Very occasionally, one of them erupts violently, changing the shape of the countryside. An example is Sakurajima (Cherry Island) in Kyushu. This volcano used to be an island in the middle of Kagoshima Bay. One day it erupted and some of the rock got so hot that it melted and poured into the sea. Gradually this rock, called lava, cooled and hardened, filling up part of the sea and making a natural roadway joining the island to the coast. Sakurajima is an island no longer.

In 1943, just south of Lake Toya in south-west Hokkaido, a new volcano appeared suddenly out of the ground. The Japanese called it Showa Shinzan (Shinzan means 'New Mountain'). Fortunately, dangerous eruptions do not happen often. Nowadays they can be predicted well in advance, and people are able to move out of the area in time.

Steam rises from the peak of Showa Shinzan.

Hot-spring resorts

There are often holiday resorts close to volcanoes because of the hot springs, where natural hot water flows out of the ground. The water contains health-giving minerals. There are many hotels and Japanese inns called *ryokan* near the springs. Often these have their own natural hot-water baths inside. The most famous hot-spring resort is Atami near Mount Fuji. It is very relaxing to spend a few days at a hotel taking a daily bath. These resorts are very popular with holiday-makers who want a short break from work.

Mount Fuji, Japan's highest mountain.

The seasons

In Japan there are four distinct seasons. The weather usually follows the same pattern every year.

Spring is quite mild. In June comes the rainy season when everyone carries an umbrella. At the end of June there are one or two violent thunderstorms, which means that summer has come! For two or three months the weather is so hot and sticky that electric fans and air-conditioners are switched on everywhere. Even businessmen use paper fans on the trains, and many people have two baths a day. Towards the end of the summer comes the typhoon season. Typhoons are dangerous storms with high winds and heavy rains that often damage houses.

Autumn days are usually clear and crisp. Then comes winter. Japan is a long, narrow country running from north to south, so the winter is much colder in the north. In Hokkaido and Tohoku (northern Honshu), the winter snowfalls begin in November. The snow may lie until April. People have to shovel it off the roofs, and dig paths through the snow to get to school or work. But in the rest of Japan winter is not so cold, and down in the south snow is a novelty.

Enjoying nature

Japanese people like to do different things according to the time of year. Summer is

▲ A spring cherry blossom-viewing picnic.

▼ The dramatic colours of autumn leaves.

too hot for picnics, so they prefer to go for trips in the spring and autumn. Every season has its special flower. March and April are the months for cherry blossom. The beautiful pink blossoms spread like a mist up the mountainside or across the park. Everywhere people sit on straw mats under the trees having picnics, chatting and singing. A favourite Japanese song is *Sakura*, 'Cherry Blossoms'.

In the autumn there are trips to see the leaves turning colour. The vivid red of maples and yellow of Japanese ginkgo trees makes an unforgettable sight which people remember in the dark winter days.

The Snow Festival

In Sapporo, the main city of Hokkaido, a Snow Festival is held every February. It is the island's biggest festival, and visitors come from all over Japan. Enormous statues are made out of ice. Sometimes the figures are famous television characters, or they might be models of famous buildings. One year they even built a Buckingham Palace out of ice!

The seasons in art

Japanese artists have always loved to paint seasonal flowers and plants such as the cherry, iris, chrysanthemum and maple. They can be seen on scrolls (long narrow pictures you can roll up), screens and even fans, tea-bowls, and *kimonos* (the traditional Japanese dress). In their homes today, Japanese people like to hang different pictures according to the season.

Poems about the seasons

In the 17th century, Japanese poets started writing poems about the seasons called *haiku*. The poems had only 17 syllables arranged in three lines of 5 – 7 – 5 syllables. Here is an example. It is about the harvest moon in September, when people often used to look at the full moon's reflection in a quiet pool.

Me-i-ge-tsu ya: i-ke o me-gu-ri-te: yo mo su-ga-ra

Under the bright moon
I walked round and round the pond
All the long night through

You could try writing a *haiku*.

Here, at the Sapporo Snow Festival, a little boy has his picture taken in front of a tram made out of ice. After the models have been carved, firemen hose them with water which freezes to make a smooth, shiny surface.

Tokyo

Tokyo became the capital of Japan in 1603, but at first it was called Edo. Edo was once a little fishing village by the River Sumida. The Shogun, Tokugawa Ieyasu, made it his capital while the Emperor stayed in the old capital of Kyoto. In 1868, the last Shogun lost his power. The Emperor came to Edo, renamed it Tokyo, and made it the capital of all Japan. The Emperor and Empress still live in the Imperial Palace surrounded by lovely gardens and a moat. Nearby is the Parliament building called the Diet.

A crowded city

During World War II, Tokyo was bombed. Most of the buildings were burned down because they were made of wood. The city was rebuilt using concrete. Now Tokyo is a modern city with almost 12 million inhabitants. Every day, many more people pour in to work in shops and offices. They often journey for over an hour to reach Tokyo, then change onto buses, undergrounds and trains. The tubes are very crowded during the rush-hour and there are station officials to push passengers onto the trains as the doors squeeze shut. In the streets there are often traffic-jams and the average speed is about 11 kilometres per hour (km/h). The monorail, a kind of train which travels on a single overhead rail, may be used more in future because it saves space. Expressways cross the city so some people have to live or work right beside a flyover. They use every last space. They even do sports and keep-fit on the flat roofs of tall buildings. Big stores have roof-top bars and children's playgrounds.

The Imperial Palace in Tokyo.

Flyovers criss-crossing in central Tokyo.

The Meiji Shrine

One of the most peaceful places in Tokyo is the Meiji Shrine, a religious building dedicated to the Emperor Meiji who reigned from 1868 to 1912. It is surrounded by a big tree-filled park. There are not many parks in Tokyo, so Tokyoites and visitors like to go to the Meiji Shrine to escape from the noise and bustle of one of the world's largest cities.

'Pedestrian paradise' on the Ginza.

A lively city

Tokyo is also a city for having fun. There are many narrow streets alive with bars and restaurants, where people go for lunch or to spend the evening. There are also museums, concert-halls, cinemas and theatres — such as the famous Kabukiza, where the colourful traditional plays called *kabuki* are performed.

Japanese people love shopping in the many department stores, or in the huge underground shopping precincts at the main stations. The shops often sell goods from abroad such as Dior fashions from France. The smartest shopping street is called the Ginza. The Kanda area is famous for its bookshops, and the stores in Akihabara sell cut-price electrical goods. Harajuku has many boutiques, and is very popular with young people who like to dance to pop music in the streets on Sundays. Some streets are closed to traffic on Sundays, so that people can enjoy shopping in safety in this so-called 'pedestrian paradise'.

Ancient capitals of Japan

Kyoto, an old capital of Japan, still preserves many ancient crafts. Master craftsmen weave fine silk called *yuzen* for *kimonos*, potters make the famous Kiyomizu pottery, and makers of fans, dolls and bamboo-ware can be found at work in their side-street shops.

Kyoto is much smaller than Tokyo, and it is easy to get up into the surrounding tree-covered hills full of quiet temples and shrines.

To the south of Kyoto is Nara, another ancient capital where the Shosoin Treasure House holds the Emperor's priceless art collection. Tame deer graze peacefully among the old buildings.

Power and industry

Japan's main problem as an industrial country is that it lacks raw material. Oil is the main source of energy, but Japan has to import 99 per cent of its supplies, mostly from Arab countries. Coal is imported from Australia, Canada and the USA. Japan wants to be more self-sufficient so it is working to save energy and to develop new kinds such as liquefied natural gas, and nuclear energy which produces 30 per cent of Japan's electricity.

Iron ore for heavy industries is also imported. Most of Japan's power stations and factories are on the very edge of the sea. This means that raw materials can go straight from ship to factory. Finished products can then go back onto the ships for distribution in Japan, or export abroad.

Hard-working robots in a car factory.

Heavy industries

Japan's Industrial Revolution started in the l9th century, but it has made most rapid progress since the 1950s. Japan is now world famous for iron and steel. It produces almost half the world's ships, and exports more cars than any other nation.

New industries

With the development of new technology, Japan is cutting back on heavy industries an building up its electronics industries. The main advantage of the new industries is that they use less raw materials and energy. Scientists are at work in the new 'science cities' such as Kansai Science City near Osaka. They are developing space projects, advanced computers, medical instruments and robots. There are even robots to help care for the sick. In most factories robotic arms are used for dangerous or repetitive work.

A giant tanker carries oil to Japan.

Companies big and small

Most workers in big companies in Japan stay in the same job all their lives. The company helps them with buying a house, holidays, education and medical expenses. In return, the workers are very loyal to their company. However, not everyone has this kind of working life. Other people work in small companies or family businesses like little grocers' shops and workshops, making things like *tatami* (ricestraw mats) or Japanese dolls.

Japanese products you might see at home.

ITEM	PRODUCED BY
Car	Toyota, Mazda, Honda, Nissan
Motorbike	Kawasaki, Honda, Suzuki
Camera	Canon, Pentax
Watch	Seiko, Citizen
Calculator	Sharp
Television/VTR	Matsushita, Hitachi, Toshiba, Sanyo
Personal stereo	Sanyo, Awia, Sony (Walkman)
Microwave	Hitachi, Sanyo

An unusual tea-lady!

Japanese industry abroad

Many Japanese firms have set up factories abroad. By 1989 there were 696 electronics factories. The Japanese use local workers paying them lower wages, especially in China and southeast Asia. This means they can make and sell goods more cheaply and compete with their foreign rivals. Now, for example, some Sony CD players have 'Made in Malaysia' written on the back, and British stores are selling Matsui VTRs made in Taiwan.

The car industry is also moving out of Japan to the USA and Europe. The most recent company to arrive in the UK is Toyota which opened a factory in Derbyshire in 1993 (see **Trade and aid,** p.31).

Pollution

During the period of rapid industrialisation, Japan was faced with problems of pollution. Factories poured waste and rubbish into the sea, poisoning fish and killing plants. Smoke and fumes made the air dirty in some industrial areas. However, since the 1970s the Government has passed many laws which have improved the situation. Now car manufacturers must make sure that cars do not give out harmful exhaust fumes. There are also strict rules about this for cars imported from abroad. Factories, too, must be more careful about getting rid of waste. One result of this is that the River Sumida is now full of fish again.

On the move

Japan has a vast and growing transport system. Millions of passengers and many tonnes of goods are carried around the country every year by land, sea and air.

By land

Japan is a mountainous country so most main routes run close to the coast. However, there is a new mountain route from Tokyo to Nagoya as well as the expressway along the coast. Another expressway runs from Nagoya to Kobe and there will soon be a route to Aomori in the far north of Honshu. These roads have tollgates at the entrance where drivers have to pay high charges to keep the roads in good repair. Tokyo to Osaka costs £70. The speed limit is 100km/h on expressways and 60km/h on other roads.

In some mountain districts special tourist roads have been built, such as the famous 'Hakone Skyline' near Mount Fuji. They

An expressway crosses a river.

are very steep and full of hairpin bends offering magnificent views across to the surrounding peaks.

In large cities where side-streets are narrow, parking is a problem. If people park outside their houses, they cause an instant traffic-jam! They have to find a parking-space off the road before they can buy a car. Bicycles are very popular for journeys to the supermarket or station.

The Shinkansen

The famous Shinkansen, or 'bullet train', ran for the first time in 1964. The new Nozomi Super-express reaches speeds of 270km/h. It links many of the main cities of Japan. The oldest branch runs from Tokyo to Osaka, Okayama, and finally to Hakata in Fukuoka, Kyushu. Two new lines opened in 1982. One crosses the country from Tokyo to Niigata, the big port on the Sea of Japan coast. The other, also from Tokyo, finishes at Morioka, 532 kilometres to the north. The whole system is controlled by computer for safety and efficiency, and it always arrives on time! There is an automatic braking system in case of earthquakes, and the newest line are specially equipped for heavy snow. Inside, the trains are very comfortable with automatic doors. Staff with trolleys move along aisles selling drinks and neatly packaged lunch boxes called 'obento'.

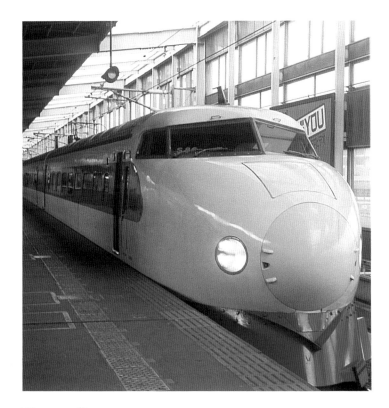

The Shinkansen, with its powerful stream-lined engine, waits at Kyoto Station. It is one of the trains run by Japa Railways Group. Shinkansen means 'New Trunk Line'.

The Maglev runs 10 centimetres above the groun

Even faster

Now an even faster way of travelling is being developed. It is called the linear motor car, or Maglev. The car uses magnets to travel smoothly and quietly just above the rails. Test runs with passengers have reached speeds of 411km/h but its record speed is 517km/h. It will come into use early next century.

By sea and air

Japan has many well-equipped harbours, so goods are carried by ship as well as by road. Passenger-boats, too, play an important part in this country of islands.

The two major international airports are Tokyo International Airport at Narita and the new Kansai Airport built on an island in Osaka Bay. It opened in September 1994. Two more runways are planned, with flights to 44 countries worldwide and 28 cities in Japan.

Fastest travelling times on the Shinkansen

ROUTE	DISTANCE	TIME
Tokyo – Osaka	515km	2hrs 30 mins
Tokyo –Hakata	1,069km	5hrs 04mins
Tokyo –Niigata	330km	1hr 32mins
Tokyo –Morioka	532km	2hrs 36mins

17

Farming, fishing and food

Most Japanese farms are very small, and farmers usually have two jobs. They work in nearby towns during the week and help on the farm at weekends. Their wives and parents do most of the regular farmwork.

On the farm

Japan has been a rice-growing country for over 2,000 years. The rice is grown in tiny paddy-fields and most farmers use mini-cultivators to make their work easier.

Japan also grows most of its vegetables and fruit. Oranges are the most popular, followed by apples and pears. Tomatoes and strawberries are grown in vinyl hothouses. The Satsuma area of Kyushu is famous for giant radishes called *daikon*.

Recently Japanese are eating more meat, eggs and dairy products, so farmers are raising larger numbers of cows, pigs and hens. They often rear them indoors because most fields are too small for grazing.

Because of lack of space to grow wheat for bread, Japan imports most of its wheat, along with maize and soybeans.

Fishing

Japanese fishing boats used to sail all over the world. However, in recent years many countries have made rules forbidding any foreign boats to fish within 320 kilometres of their coasts. The Japanese must now fish mainly in their own coastal waters. To make

Freshly-caught octopus at Tsukiji Fish Market in Tokyo.

18

up for this they are importing fish from Russia and the USA. Fish-farming is also being developed. Fish such as shrimps and salmon are bred in a special area of the sea or in a river.

The Japanese often eat their fish raw. So at Tsukiji fish market in Tokyo, trains run into the middle of the market to whisk the fish off round the country while it is still fresh.

Food and drink

Japan produces most of its own food and Japanese people like to eat at least one Japanese-style meal a day, usually in the evening. However, they also eat many foreign foods. For breakfast they might have cereal with bacon and eggs, toast and coffee, and for lunch a quick hamburger or spaghetti. When the Japanese go to a bar for a drink they often choose whisky or beer which, these days, is probably made in Japan.

Some families eat traditionally sitting on floor cushions. Today it is 'curry-rice'.

Japanese favourites

Japanese cooks use soya sauce (made from soya beans), *sake* (rice wine) and sugar. Seaweed is also used. A favourite dish is *sukiyaki*, cooked in a big bowl in the middle of the table. Steaming slices of beef and vegetables are taken from the bowl and dipped in raw egg. *Tempura* consists of fish and vegetables fried in crispy batter, and dipped in a sauce containing grated *daikon*. The most popular raw fish dish is *sushi*. Slices of tuna, salmon, mackerel, squid, octopus and prawns are served on rice with strong mustard and ginger. Most meals also include rice, soup and pickles washed down with *sake*, followed by fruit and green tea. Noodles (a kind of Japanese spaghetti) are very popular as a quick snack.

Table manners

During a meal, Japanese people eat out of several small bowls of different shapes and sizes. They use chopsticks — two wooden or bamboo sticks held in the right hand — to carry the food into their mouths. They hold the bowl in the left hand while eating with the right. Noodles can be eaten with a loud slurping noise!

Home and family

Most Japanese people would like to own their own home but, because building land is scarce, houses are expensive. Most houses are quite small with two floors and a tiny garden. Many people live in blocks of rented flats called *danchi*.

Old houses

In the past, all Japanese houses were built of wood. They had sliding inner doors covered with paper, sliding windows, and rain-shutters and overhanging eaves for protection against rain and snow. People did not have chairs and beds. Instead they sat on cushions on *tatami* (rice-straw mats), and ate from low tables. At night they brought out very thick mattresses and quilts from the cupboards, and spread them on the floor for sleeping. They could use just one room for sitting-room, dining-room and bedroom. Nowadays there are few of these really old houses left, found mainly in country districts.

Modern living

Modern houses still have a wooden frame but this is covered with concrete as a protection from fire. Most new houses have

An old-style house in the country. It is raised off the ground to keep it dry and warm in winter and cool in summer, and it faces south. The house has a thatched roof.

A typical modern house with a small garden.

one or two rooms in the old style with *tatami,* sliding-doors and a *tokonoma* (an alcove with a picture-scroll and flowers). However, the other rooms have carpets, dining-table and chairs, sofa, armchairs and a TV set. The kitchen has a cooker, freezer, fridge, electric rice-cooker, and many modern utensils. Upstairs, some modern bedrooms have beds and there are often bunk-beds for the children.

Family life

Most Japanese families have a mother, father and one or two children. In the past it was the custom for a young married couple to live with the husband's parents. Nowadays, they usually live separately, although the old people are often close by, so that the young ones can look after them.

In many families, the father leaves home early and returns from work late, so the children do not see him very often. However, some men try to spend more time with their families. The mother is usually in charge of the household budget. She does not normally go out to work herself until the children are older. She looks after them,

encouraging them in their schoolwork and making sure that they do their homework.

As the children grow up, their mother teaches them good manners, such as how to use chopsticks properly, and how to bow politely when they meet other people. (The Japanese do not shake hands.) The children also learn to take their shoes off when they arrive home. Their slippers are ready one step up from the door. In a *tatami* room, they have to go barefoot. They must keep the *tatami* spotlessly clean for sitting and sleeping on. They must also use special plastic shoes for the toilet.

Bathtime

The Japanese like to take a bath every day. The bathrooms have two parts. On one side is the tub full of steaming hot water. Next to it is a small space with taps, plastic bowls and stools. here they sit and wash themselves with plenty of soap and water. When they are quite clean, they climb into the tub. They sit up to the chin in water just relaxing. Because they have already washed themselves, the water stays clean so the next person can use the same water. Not all houses have their own bathroom and many people go to a public bath. They enjoy bathing together and chatting, though men and and women usually have separate baths.

Children and schools

Japanese children have to go to school from the age of six to fifteen, but most of them stay on until they are eighteen. Many children also go to nursery school.

The school year starts in April with a big ceremony. There are lessons from 8.30 am to 3.30 pm Monday to Friday – *and* on most Saturdays! The classes usually have about forty children. The Japanese like to work together in groups, and they start learning how to do this in their classes at school. The children are proud of their class and often write their own classroom rules, making sure that everyone obeys them. There are various customs at Japanese schools, like changing into indoor shoes, bowing to the teacher, eating lunch in the classroom with the teacher, and staying after school to clean the classrooms and playground.

At primary school, children learn Japanese, mathematics, social studies, science, art, music, and games. At secondary school, most of them learn English. Many Japanese children have extra lessons out of school to help them with difficult subjects.

School outings

Children always look forward to school journeys. In the spring term, year-groups learn about their country by visiting the many historic sites such as the Great Shrine at Nikko. In the summer holidays they go away to the mountains or the sea. Best of all, the children enjoy the chance to spend

A whole class learns the electric organ.

Enjoying a packed lunch.

It is Girls' Day so this little girl serves special drinks in front of the display of dolls. The children are wearing traditional dress for this occasion.

Boys' Day carp streamers.

time together with their friends, often staying for a few days in a *ryokan*.

Free time

Japanese children have various hobbies and pastimes. They love watching TV which has seven main channels. There are many children's programmes, even at breakfast time, with cartoons about Superman and spacemen. Children also like playing all kinds of computer games very much. They like reading books and comics and making models, including *origami* – folding paper models. Many primary school children have piano and violin lessons. Others spend time caring for the family pets. There are not many parks and playgrounds, but children like to get outside to practise baseball and football or go on bicycle rides with their friends.

Children's festivals

There are two special days for all children in Japan. March 3rd is Girls' Day. Mothers and daughters display a set of dolls dressed as the Emperor and Empress with their courtiers. They are sometimes very old and valuable. The girls dress in their best clothes, and invite their friends for special food and drinks in front of the dolls.

Boys' Day is on May 5th. It is a national holiday. Indoors they display a set of *samurai* dolls (see p. 27) in the *tokonoma*. In the garden they fly carp streamers called *koinobori* from a pole. There is a different-sized streamer for every boy in the family with a tiny one for a baby. The carp is a river fish which swims strongly up the stream. Parents hope their sons will be brave like the carp, boldly facing the dangers of life.

Religion and festivals

There are two main religions in Japan: Shinto and Buddhism. Most Japanese people belong to both. There are also about one million Christians.

Shinto

Shinto is found only in Japan. The word *Shinto* means 'the Way of the Gods'. People used to believe that there were gods living in the mountains, trees and all natural things. Today this belief is not so strong, but the colourful ceremonies of Shinto are still enjoyed. Every summer, people carry a shrine to the top of Mount Fuji and ask the god to protect climbers from danger. Cleanliness is important in Shinto and people have to rinse their hands and mouths at a stone basin when they visit a shrine. The shrine gate, called a *torii*, is usually painted red. Shinto is a religion for happy occasions like births and weddings.

Buddhism

Buddhism was started in India over 2,000 years ago by an Indian prince. He gave up the luxury of the court to try to find everlasting peace through a simple, thoughtful way of life. In Buddhism there are no gods to worship, but most temples have a statue of the Buddha. Buddhists pay great respect to their ancestors and think about life after death. Funerals are usually held at Buddhist temples.

A famous Buddha statue at Kamakura.

Shrines and temples

In Shinto and Buddhism, people do not go to worship every week. They can go to a shrine or temple whenever they want.

Kyoto and Nara, two ancient capitals of Japan, are full of temples and shrines, with lovely gardens. The famous garden at Ryoanji is made only of sand and rocks, which look like islands sticking out of the sea. Todaiji is the biggest wooden building in the world. Inside there is a statue of the Buddha, 15 metres high. Horyuji is the oldest wooden building in the world, dating from AD 607. (*Ji* means 'temple'.)

Festival time

The Japanese year is full of festivals based on religion. Many are spectacular with processions in the streets. The Gion Festival in Kyoto commemorates a plague in AD 869. August is the time for the Bon Festival, which is Japanese Hallowe'en or All Saints. People remember their ancestors and celebrate by dancing in the open air.

The most important festival is Shogatsu (New Year) from January 1st to 3rd. Everyone has a holiday. Houses are decorated with pine and bamboo. On New Year's Eve, the temple bell tolls solemnly across the countryside. The next day, everyone wishes each other '*Akemashite omedeto*' (A Happy New Year!). People feast on special food such as *mochi* (rice cakes). The holiday is a time for family visits and going to the shrine. Women like to wear their best *kimonos* for this occasion.

Crowds visit the Meiji Shrine for Shogatsu.

The kimono

The *kimono* is the traditional dress of the Japanese — both for women and men. It is usually made of silk with a wide sash called an *obi*, but in the heat of summer light cotton *kimonos*, called *yukata*, are more comfortable. Most Japanese people have western-style clothes for everyday wear, but for special occasions they still like to dress traditionally. *Yukata* are also popular with men for relaxing at home after work, and at hot-spring resorts.

The *kimono* has a very simple shape made up of wide strips of cloth sewn together. Designs are woven, embroidered, dyed and painted on the cloth. Use the shape in the picture to design a *kimono* using the flowers of your favourite season.

Sports and pastimes

Although most Japanese people work long hours they like to make the most of their leisure. Housewives, too, try to make time for hobbies outside the home. Sport and travel are favourite pastimes.

In 1995 over 10 million Japanese people had holidays abroad. However, most Japanese spend their holidays travelling inside Japan. In 1987 the government passed the Resort Bill to encourage the development of new holiday resorts all over the country.

A choice of sports

Many people prefer traditional sports known as 'martial arts'. The most popular traditional spectator sport is *sumo* (wrestling). The wrestlers weigh over 150 kilograms. The aim is to throw your opponent out of the ring, or to make him overbalance. The spectators get very excited as they wait for the wrestlers to go for the attack. Often the fight itself is over in a few seconds. There are six big contests

Two *sumo* wrestlers face each other in the ring. The matches were originally held in Shinto shrines so the referee is dressed like a Shinto priest.

every year in Tokyo, Nagoya, Osaka and Fukuoka which are televised daily.

Some Japanese prefer sports from abroad. Tennis and golf are very popular. In the winter thousands of people go to the mountains for winter sports. Baseball is still popular, but football is the newest craze. With fourteen teams in the J-League, Japan aims to play in the World Cup 2002.

Pastimes, old and new

Japanese people have a wide choice of hobbies. There are special Japanese pastimes as well as those from abroad.

Ikebana is the Japanese way of arranging flowers. Only a few flowers are used. There are always three main stems in the arrangement, one for Heaven, one for Earth and one for Man. Many women and girls learn *ikebana*, although the teachers are often old men who have studied all their lives. Other people, especially old folk, like to grow *bonsai* (miniature trees).

The tea ceremony is a very formal way of making tea and serving it to a handful of guests. Everything is spotlessly clean and only the most beautiful utensils and tea-bowls are used. The host and guests behave in a quiet and thoughtful way. The tea ceremony creates a moment of peace in the bustle of everyday life.

Many people are interested in traditional Japanese plays and music. Today they also watch American and European plays and films. They are fond of the music of Bach and Beethoven, and other famous western composers. Housewives often sing their music in the local housewives' chorus. In the popular *karaoke* bars businessmen sing their favourite popsongs to a recorded backing.

Host and guests at a Tea Ceremony.

Martial arts and samurai warriors

Some of the most popular martial arts in Japan today are *kendo* (fencing), *kyudo* (archery), *judo*, *aikido* and *karate* (forms of self defence without weapons). They are also practised in many other countries of the world. The martial arts have developed from skills used in battle by the *samurai* warriors of Japan's Feudal Age (1192-1868), when the Shoguns were in power. *Samurai* means 'one who serves', and the *samurai* always fought loyally and bravely for their lords. After 1868, when the *samurai* class was abolished, the martial arts were encouraged as a sport for ordinary people. Self-control has always been an important part of the martial arts, and even today a practice session often starts with a period of meditation, or silent thought, to train the mind.

Words and writing

Japan is the only country in the world where Japanese is spoken. Sometimes it is quite difficult for foreigners to work in Japan, and for the Japanese to move abroad, because they must learn each other's languages.

Japanese writing

Japan is across the sea from China. Chinese people were writing about 4,000 years ago. For a long time the Japanese only spoke their language and did not write it down, but in about AD 500 they started to use Chinese letters to write Japanese. These Chinese letters were like pictures of things. They have changed now, but some of them still look like pictures and you can guess what they mean. Japanese children have to learn at least 2,000 Chinese letters called *kanji* at school. They also have to learn two sets of forty-six Japanese signs. One set is used for word-building and sentence-building, and the other is for writing foreign words.

Brush or biro

In the past, Japanese people used to write with a special writing brush. It had a handle made of bamboo and bristles made of different animals' hair, such as squirrel or sheep. For a really big brush they used horse or even wolf hair. Today most people write with fountain pens or biros, but they

Calligraphy practice.

28

like to use brushes for legal papers, certificates and New Year cards.

Calligraphy

All children start learning to use brushes at school when they are about ten. Some continue with brush-writing or 'calligraphy' in their art lessons. Adults often carry on with it as their main hobby.

Calligraphy is done with special ink in a solid block. It is made of soot mixed with glue. The writer pours water onto an ink-stone, then rubs the ink-block to and fro on the stone. The block dissolves in the water making a pool of black ink. The writing paper is very thin but strong. Japanese writing usually goes from top to bottom and from right to left.

Each line must be written in the proper order. Pupils have to think carefully before they write. They are not allowed to paint over the lines if they go wrong. So calligraphy teaches the Japanese to be thoughtful and careful, and improves their everyday handwriting.

Reading downwards, this says *SHU-JI* 'calligraphy'.

Some Japanese words for you to use

The Japanese do not use the Roman alphabet, but we have used it here to help you to say the words easily.

Ohayo gozaimasu = Good morning.

Say it bit by bit like this:
O-ha-yo go-za-i-ma-su
Then try saying it altogether again quickly:
Ohayo gozaimasu!

Do the same with these words.
Hai (Ha-i) = Yes
Iie (I-i-e) = No
Konnichi wa (Ko-n-ni-chi wa) = Hallo
Ogenki desu ka (O-ge-n-ki de-su ka) = How are you?
Hai, genki desu (Ha-i, ge-n-ki de-su) = I am fine
Onamae wa nan desu ka (O-na-ma-e wa na-n de-su ka) = What is your name?
Lisa desu (Lisa de-su) = It's Lisa
Arigato (A-ri-ga-to) = Thank you
Sayonara (Sa-yo-na-ra) = Goodbye

Kanji
Some Japanese *kanji* for you to guess. (Clue: they are all things you can see in the countryside.)

	Old *kanji*	New *kanji*
1.	⛰	山
2.	巛	川
3.	木	木

Answers:

1. Mountain (*yama*) 2. River (*kawa*) 3. Tree (*ki*)

29

Japan and the world

For most of its long history Japan has been at peace with the rest of the world. However, in the first half of the 20th century it increased its military strength and tried to build an empire starting with its neighbours, Korea and China. In 1941 Japan entered the Pacific War (World War II), fighting against the USA and its allies. The war ended in disaster for the Japanese when, in August 1945, the Americans dropped atomic bombs on the cities of Hiroshima and Nagasaki. The cities were destroyed, thousands of people were killed, and Japan surrendered.

Keeping the peace

After the war the allies gave Japan a set of rules, called a Constitution, telling them how to rule the country as a democracy like the USA and most Western countries. One of these rules forbids them to attack another country. So Japan has only Self-Defence Forces and is completely opposed to nuclear weapons. At the Peace Park and Museum in Hiroshima people from all over the world join the Japanese to remember the atomic bombs and to pray for peace. Japan tries to keep friendly ties with every country and is an active member of the United Nations. Japan sent Ground Self-Defence Forces to join UN peace-keeping operations at the end of the Gulf War. Japan also helps with international refugee work.

This is the ruined International Trade Fair building in Hiroshima which was almost destroyed in 1945 when the atomic bomb fell. It is now kept as a memorial called the A-bomb Dome.

An economic giant

During the 1950s and 1960s Japan worked hard at rebuilding its industries. It surprised the world by its rapid progress. Now as an economic power Japan is on equal terms with the leading nations of the world. Today, however, progress is not as fast as it used to be and Japan shares many problems with other industrialised countries. As the Pacific Basin Region (all those countries surrounding the Pacific Ocean) becomes more important, Japan also hopes to play a leading role there.

Trade and aid

Japan's trading vessels go all over the world. Its main trading partner is the USA. Asia is also a very important trading area. Sometimes there is 'trade friction' when its trading partners complain that Japan is selling too much and not buying enough. Japan is trying to close this 'trade gap' by setting up more factories abroad, and by making it easier for foreign countries to export to Japan.

As a rich nation, Japan plays its part in supporting countries in need, especially in Asia and Africa. The Japanese send money and a variety of experts to teach and advise. For example, Japanese farming experts recently went to Bangladesh to assist with new research projects.

Open to the world

In 1989 Emperor Hirohito died after a reign of 63 years. At the new Emperor Akihito's coronation there were special guests from nearly every country, including the Prince and Princess of Wales.

The Japan of Emperor Akihito is keener

Japanese study with their English teacher.

than ever to share ideas and knowledge with the rest of the world. Japanese and foreign scientists work together on basic research projects. The Japanese government invites hundreds of English teachers to Japan every year to work in its schools, and more and more foreigners are learning Japanese. Japanese actors and musicians perform all over the world, and in 1994, the writer, Oe Kenzaburo, won the famous Nobel Prize in Literature.

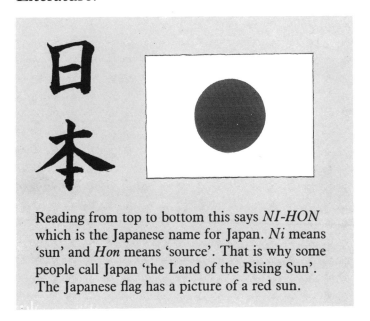

Reading from top to bottom this says *NI-HON* which is the Japanese name for Japan. *Ni* means 'sun' and *Hon* means 'source'. That is why some people call Japan 'the Land of the Rising Sun'. The Japanese flag has a picture of a red sun.

Index and summary

Area:	377,780 square kilometres
Population:	Nearly 25 million
Main islands:	Honshu Hokkaido, Kyushu, Shikoku
Other regional names:	Tohoku, Chuba, Kanto, Chugoku, Kinki
Capital:	Tokyo
Main towns:	Yokohama; Osaka, Nagoya. Sapporo, Kobe, Kyoto, Fukuoki, Kawasaki, Hiroshima, Kitakyushu
Main exports:	Machinery, cars, iron and steel, chemicals, optical instruments, video tape recorders
Main imports:	Oil, petroleum products, foodstuffs, raw materials machinery chemicals textiles
Main crop:	Rice
Highest point:	Mount Fuji, 3,776 metres
Longest river:	Shinano, 367 kilometres
Official language:	Japanese
Currency:	Yen
Airlines:	Japan Airlines, All Nippon Airways, Japan Air System